To Hell and Beyond

by

Guy McAnally

Empyrion Press

PO Box 140914

Broken Arrow OK 74014

Contents

Acknowledgements

I would like to thank my wife Barbara, for putting up with me; also my daughters, Misty, Tonia, and Amber. The Lord knows we've had some hard times; my sons-in-law Chris, Josh, and Fortino; also my son Guy Jr. and his wife Alisha, who are all now saved and filled with the Spirit of God.

Thanks to my sisters, Patti, Linda, and especially Sandy and her husband Jim for being there for me through all the bad years of my life. They have been grandparents to my kids and my nineteen grandchildren; also Gary my hot rod brother-in-law. He has always been a good husband and father; my nieces and nephews, Mary, Michelle, Jason, and Brandy; my friends Bobby, Edd the Christian poet (He's got a poetry book coming out next year), and my best friend Scott for always having words of encouragement, like Edd.

I knew these guys on the other side of the fence. Now we are all serving God and seeing the Kingdom grow by leaps and bounds. Edd started a men's ministry with four others at his church. Scott and I joined in a year and a half ago, and now we are feeding breakfast to close to one hundred guys once a month. Can you see what God is doing? AMEN!

Acknowledgements

Thank you Billy Joe and Sharon Daugherty for all that you do in the ministry, for the millions that you have helped.

Thanks to the prophets for inspiring me to write this book.

Thank you Jesus, without you none of this was possible.

Jeremiah 29:11 says, "For I know the thoughts I have towards you saith the Lord, thoughts of peace and not of evil, with an expected end". He wants us to have hope. He says in the Bible that He knows the end from the beginning. It also says that He knew us while we were still in our mother's womb.

Did I hear you say that's personal? That's what Jesus wants, a personal relationship with YOU. He's omnipresent and omnipotent. He is right there in that room with you. He's ready. Are you ready?

Say "yes" to Jesus today; or read my book first. Then you will be ready.

Thank you, readers for buying my book. It is my prayer that the Lord will speak to you and help you as He did me in a powerful way. I pray that you will get involved in ministry.

Jesus said that the fields are plenty, and the harvest has never been more important than now.

You see, this drug "meth", they tell me is all the way down to some grade schools, where gang violence is corrupting our kids and sending them to an early grave. I have a nephew that lost his life at nineteen. Before that, he had come to church and was okay with God. Somehow, his life was cut short.

There were three hundred kids at his funeral. Pastor John preached the funeral and gave a call for salvation. There were hands raised all over the building. I was amazed and so glad that my nephew had followed the Lord's call, so he didn't die in vain.

Sometimes the devil steals a loved one and God will show up and turn it around for good. That will make you get up early and pray for your kids. Remember, Satan is said to be the god of this world. He comes to steal, kill, and destroy you and your family. He wants you busted and disgusted. Please don't let him devour you. Stand up for your rights. Tell him you are covered with the shed blood of Jesus Christ. Tell him you have salvation in Christ your redeemer. Don't be lukewarm. Be fired up for Jesus! Amen…

Acknowledgements

Well, I'm starting to preach. I'm forgetting that you have a book to read.

Love and grace to the sinner because that's where I came from.

To the saints, I have one word for you. Don't just be a warmer of the pew. Get up and fight the good fight. Our young people are dying at an alarming rate. Have you told two people about Jesus today?

I used to carry a knife, now I carry a two edged sword, the King James Bible. Get you one. It's a must read.

Ephesians 6:11-24 is a prayer written to you. Read it every day. Get it down in your spirit. When you can recite it, you are more than a conqueror. It's about putting on that armor...

I could go on, but you have a book to read. My prayers go to you, from the writer.

Introduction

This book is a true testimony of the hand of God on my life. You will read how God dispatched His angels at the right time; and how drugs were taking me to HELL over a thirty-six year period, and I never saw it coming.

I didn't know God, but I had gone to church as a child and I knew a few pastors through the years, but that wasn't enough to keep me out of HELL.

An overdose of a killer drug that plagues our streets today, CHRYSTAL METH, sent me over the edge, into a spiraling out of body experience like I had never seen before. I documented every minute that I went through for a three day period, with the devil first, then an angel, and finally God speaking to me, outlining for me the path I was to take; a path that I followed.

Read how a 250 pound mad man, that used to be so quick to fly off the handle, could end up with such patience. I even amaze myself sometimes. Thank you, Jesus.

I was born 09-25-1952. I'm 56 years old. Today's date is 05-15-2009. This traumatic experience happened March 17, 2000. It's been over 9 years ago.

Introduction

I was born to loving parents, Doyle and Mary McAnally. Life is good when you're young. My parents were both on the Tulsa Police Department. As a matter of fact, my mother was one of the first police women in town.

As I grew up, I saw a lot that was wrong with my life, but I was having fun. I had friends like Bobby, who were going to church and acting well. His dad owned a Ford dealership in Broken Arrow. He was one of the only good influences I had in my life. He always did well in school, just a stand up guy. Thank you Bobby for what you contributed in my life.

I hate to say it, but the rest of my friends were heathens like me, so I lost my good friend Bobby, because I began smoking and he was an athlete. Sorry Bobby, I should have followed you. If I did, maybe now *I* would have two car dealerships, and I too would be giving every time I turn around. Yeah buddy, word gets around. Yes, God has blessed him.

Now Mike on the other hand, smoked, cussed, and I don't know what all. He was over one day. We were playing in the barn. He pulled out his smokes and fired one up. I told him to watch it, putting it out in the hay. You see, my sister Linda had all of her ribbons and trophies in the tack room. Her diamond studded saddle was in there too.

Introduction

We got thirsty and headed in for some refreshments. We were in the house about thirty minutes when my other sister, Sandy, screamed, "My God, the barn's on fire!"

I always told them it wasn't me, but they knew. I really felt bad. Mike wasn't allowed over any more. I really don't know what happened to him. We got a new barn built, but then I got a new go cart and more friends that smoked.

I think you are getting it now. Smoking brought foul language. That brought drinking. That brought fighting. All of that brought drug use. On and on and on, and I'm not even in junior high yet.

My story starts at 14 years of age…

Chapter 1

The School Years

At the age of fourteen, I was drinking beer, liquor, smoking pot, having wild parties, and even had hash and acid.

My mom had left my Dad. They divorced and she moved away to Beaumont, Texas. My father was an alcoholic, and had a lot of women around all of the time. My older sisters had married by the time mom and dad separated.

Mom passed away at the age of 48 from cancer.

My dad worked at a Chevy dealership and brought home some cool cars for me to drive. There were Camaros, Chevelles, and brand new hot rods.

I had a job, so I had money. Once at the age of fifteen, I put gas in the car and head out for a night on the town. The only license I had was a motorcycle license. My dad and I had a deal. He would turn his head and hope I didn't get caught.

I was peeling the tires, pulling out of the Manhattan Pool Hall parking lot; and an off-duty police officer caught me. He just happened to know my dad. He called my dad from a pay phone, and my Dad's girlfriend drove him down to get the car.

Of course my Dad told him I had stolen the car, and that he would see that I was punished. Dad told me I couldn't drive anymore.

The very next week, I begged him, reminding him that he would have the house to himself.

A friend of mine had moved to Bartlesville, and lived right on the 18th hole of the golf course. His mom had married a rich man, so every weekend we would go to Bartlesville. We had beer, liquor, pot, hash, pills, and eventually cocaine.

I got a job at a radio shop at the age of sixteen. I began to acquire quite a bad record for drag racing, burning rubber, and running red lights. My dad knew someone at the DMV, so they gave me lots of chances. I did lose my license twice, and my dad got it back for me both times.

Working at the radio shop, I made a lot of money because I was fast. A lot of the customers were pimps and drug dealers. They knew to leave party favors in the seat for a good and fast installation. I would get to keep the trade-in equipment, and I would sell them at school. I always had a suspicion that they were hot.

One night it all came to an end. Yes, I got caught with pot, pills, booze, and hot stereos. Wow! Seventeen years old, and going to jail.

The judge told me that he was tired of seeing police officer's sons like me. I was too young for the military, so he asked me to leave the state.

I had a married sister, Patti, who lived in Pueblo, Colorado. She was strict. No smoking. No drinking and I had to go to church and school. I didn't have many credits because I goofed off so much. My sister had a friend at church who knew how to deal with drop outs, and I really wanted to get back on track.

I went to school at 6:30 a.m. and got out at 2:30 p.m., and still got seven credits. I got a two credit work release, and two days a week I attended vo-tech at the small engine repair academy of Southern Colorado College, so I had to pass all of this.

My sister was all set on me graduating my senior year with 21 or 22 credits, but soon I was back in Tulsa. A lot of my friends had dropped out of school, and some were now deceased. It was amazing how many of them were gone.

I spent my senior year at Rogers High School, and got a good job working on cars. I was also building a motorcycle on the side. My work release was at a bike shop, a Yamaha dealer. I worked on a lot of snowmobiles, since we were the only bike shop that worked on them.

I graduated from Rogers in 1970 and had a kid the next year. She will be 38 on her next birthday. I haven't seen her in years.

Chapter 2

After Graduation

My dad and I went to Florida to do pipeline work, and make some big money. That of course, meant big time partying. I was drinking and doing drugs and working 12 to 14 hours a day. I had noticed and older guy, one of the superintendents, was able to party a lot, and I asked him how he did it. That is when I was introduced to black mollies. That meant I could party for days without end.

One night I went home after a night of partying and decided to do the dishes. I stuck my hand in a glass, and it broke. I almost cut my finger off. I had cut a vein, and there was blood everywhere. I went next door to ask if I needed to go to the hospital. A little old lady about 70 years of age answered the door, and I told her what I had done.

She said, "Let me see, Honey".

I took the towel off, and she fainted.

Her husband came running down the hall, looked down at her and said, "Now look what you've done, of course you need a doctor".

I went to the hospital, and they said my heart was beating too fast, and I had lost a lot of blood.

I told them I didn't know why my heart was beating so fast. Then, a doctor came in asking me about drugs and speed, so I confessed.

He said he wouldn't tell. He sewed me up, and I was off and running. He told me I would have to stay off of drugs until my hand was healed up, so I did. I only smoked pot.

I ended up living in a small town on the Alabama-Florida state line. They had only one bar in that town. It was right across from the jail, which was a large portable building with only four cells.

The cops were nice. They were always in the bar. Before you got in your car they would escort you across the street and charge you $50 for public drunk, and you wouldn't get your car towed in.

Everyone called the jail, the Hilton. I probably visited there about 15 or 20 times. They had a good bed and lots of good hot coffee. They would never let you be late for work. That turned out to be a good deal.

I should have had a lot of money when I left that job. I only saved about $10,000. I know some of the guys had saved $50,000. Of course, they went to the places on the coast that had seafood and fancy drinks. They also drove new cars. I had pretty nice cars too, and finally got me a new one, a 1973 Plymouth Sebring.

I got another new one when I met my wife in 1979. We got married. Her name was Barbra.

Our first date was a Merle Haggard concert, where we leaned on a tree, and smoked pot with 4 or 5 other people.

Barbra had two little girls, and a year later we had a son. We named him Guy Jr. She had to quit her job because they started to screen their workers.

I started working a lot of hours so I could afford a place to live, a car, pot, and cocaine. By that time I was free basing, living in a small trailer house, and driving an old pickup truck. My car had been repossessed.

I think I made $43,000 that year, and couldn't afford $160 a month car payment. We were spending about $160 on our land, a $200 trailer payment, and $130 a month on bills. Anyway, it was less than $500 a month, and we still couldn't live on the $500 a week I was bringing home, so Barbra had to get a job working for my sister. We were selling drugs by that time too, and making a total of about $900 a week.

We ended up losing everything, and moved in with Barbra's sister. That didn't last too long, and we saved enough to move out. We moved into a house down the street from Barbra's job. I would take her to work, and she would walk home.

Everything was going along fine. Then she got pregnant.

I thought, "This can't happen. I can't afford this".

My sister, Sandy pulled me aside and had a talk with me. She said it was time to slack off of the drugs. She made good money at that time, and took us to the hospital in her new car when our daughter, Amber, was born.

Sandy told me how much money she made. It was about half of what I made, and *she* had a nice home and new car.

We bought a new 16' by 85' mobile home, a really nice home on wheels. I was still making good money, and going out of town to work. I still had to work a lot of hours in order to afford our habits, and drive a better car.

Are you getting the picture by now?

I was playing pool, professionally, and gambling. I was always lucky, so I made more and more money while doing more drugs.

As the kids got older, they knew everything that was going on, and soon, *they* were bringing drugs into my house.

One day, the district attorney visited me and said he knew my dad. He said that my son-in-law was dealing drugs. Of course I knew it. He was giving a lot of drugs to me, just so he could stay at my house. I had a couple of pounds of crank in my closet.

This man was a 32nd degree Mason who belonged to my dad's lodge. He could easily have busted me, but he didn't. He gave me 24 hours to get my son-in-law out of the house, so I told my son-in-law what the district attorney had said.

It was a real awakening. I would not get in my car with any kind of drugs. I stopped dealing, but not using. In fact I went to work out of town, and was using more and more.

My wife would send me whatever I needed. She was getting my checks, and I was making $800 to $1000 a week for 80 hours of work.

Chapter 3

My Dad

By 1998, I was racing a truck at a drag strip where you could race pickups.

My dad called me up one Saturday at about 1:00 p.m. and said, "Hi Son. I would like you to come over. There are some things that I need to get straight with you. I know that I can trust you".

I said, "Where are you going?".

He said, "You know".

I told him, "Don't talk like that, Dad".

I failed to tell you that he had found the Lord. I had just been to his house on that Wednesday to put up a ceiling fan. He was humming and whistling gospel songs, and making me real uneasy. He was always watching Billy Graham and Benny Hinn. If you don't know who they are, I will pray for you.

My dad always wanted to pray for me. He had told me that when he was in the hospital on his death bed, everyone had counted him out, except Jesus. He had been living the wrong life for 67 years.

Jesus told him he could either, pray with the hospital chaplain and go home; or he could read the Word, attend to its sayings, and have ten more years.

He chose to read and live God's Word, and that he did. He could read through the Bible in three months. He documented every time, what he had read. He had a photographic memory. He witnessed to many people after that. He would meet a lot of people, because he owned a used car lot. He sat in the same seat every Sunday in church.

I was working on my truck when he called, and I said that I would be over there at about 2:00.

He said "ok", then called again asking if I could hurry. He didn't talk like there was anything wrong.

I was washing my hands, and looked up and saw my dad's pastor coming up my driveway. As he got out of his car, I knew somehow, that something had happened.

I said, "Did my dad pass?".

He said, "Yes he did".

He told me that my dad had called him at 10:00 the night before, saying that "The angels are standing at the foot of my bed, and they will be back to get me tomorrow".

I went to my dad's house with the pastor. My dad was lying on the couch. He had been watching Benny Hinn, but he wasn't facing the television. He was looking straight up at Heaven with this big smile on his face.

What a way to go!

You see, Pastor John was in that hospital room ten years earlier. The doctor had said that if my dad goes out or dies again, they would not be able to resuscitate him. My dad was in I.C.U. with tubes everywhere. Pastor John said for us to join hands and pray. He prayed loud. Other people were watching.

All of a sudden, a bolt of fire shot through me, and I hit the bars of the bed with my knees. As I got back up, my dad came out of the coma.

The doctor had said that, because my dad had a stroke, he would be paralyzed on one side of his body. The first he did when he awoke was to start pulling tubes from his body.

He sat up and said, "Son, who is running the car lot?"

That was him, always worrying about his business.

I was clueless. I didn't know what had happened. I do know that he drove himself to the car lot three days later and went to work.

Every time I went by there, he would say, "I am praying for you, Son. Could you come to church with me?"

What a work God had done with my dad. He wasn't the grouch who used to cuss me. He was way too happy. If somebody bought a car and blew the motor, my dad would take it back and give them another one.

Before, he would have thrown them off of the lot, and said a few choice words in the process.

So my dad passed away, and I was sorry that I wasn't there for him. He had always been there for me.

He didn't owe anyone anything. There were no records for the payments owed him from all of the cars that he financed for people. He had done something with the records, giving his customers their cars just for being faithful.

God was faithful to him, giving him the best ten years of his life. My dad had lung disease, but he hardly used oxygen at all during the last two years. It was like he was healed, which was weird to me.

After all of that, I still kept getting high. I did stop smoking the year my dad died. It was 1998. Slowly, I turned back to my old ways, and began to smoke pot and do crank…

Chapter 4

When Christians Pray

In early 2000, I was working for a backhoe service. Since I was the swimming pool digger, a co-worker named Fred if I could dig a pool for Camp Victory on Keystone Lake. He was a Christian biker dude who attended church at Victory Christian Center.

I replied in an obnoxious voice, "That will be the way I pay my tithes".

So I loaded up on a Saturday morning, to dig a pool at Camp Victory. When I arrived, I was shocked to see how nice this retreat camp really was. It was right on the water, a place where kids and adults could have Christian fun in the sun.

I was digging the pool, and at about lunch time, Fred came to me and said, "Hey, let's eat".

I told him that I had my lunch in the truck. He knew that I had more than lunch in the truck.

As I headed toward my truck I heard him yell, "Goulash, Man!"

Do you like goulash? It happens to be my favorite.

Fred put his arm around my shoulder, and turned me towards the lunch room. As we entered the large fellowship hall, I could smell the food. There were kids everywhere. We headed for the lunch line. I got my food, sat down and started eating.

That's when Fred grabbed my arm and said, "Hold it Man. We're going to pray".

I replied, "Well get it on".

He said, "No. Pastor Billy Joe is coming in to pray".

So we waited. Pastor Billy Joe Daugherty prayed and prayed, and I became about half sick, because he pointed and said, "I pray for the construction crew that is out here digging our pool".

At that point, food really didn't taste that good. We got through eating, and I headed toward my truck. Fred stayed with me so that I couldn't indulge in what I wanted to. So I went to finish the pool dig.

As I was working that afternoon, I looked up and there was Billy Joe, the co-pastor, Fred, and some other guy praying and pointing. I backed out of their way, and their fingers just followed me. I felt trapped. I wasn't ready.

I finished digging the pool, and found out later that pastor Billy Joe had asked Fred if I was saved, and Fred told him that I was a heathen. I loaded the backhoe, and headed home.

Fred shouted at me on the radio, "God's going to get you some day".

I answered with a hollow, "10-4".

I was really under conviction. All of this happened two weeks before I went to Hell.

Chapter 5

Hell

On March 17, 2000, I had just come from Minnesota. I had driven all night and got home at about 6:00 a.m. I was out of pot and crank, and had been up for four days.

At 2:00 p.m., I got up and took a shower, then got on the phone to find some stuff. I called a friend, and he said to give him a couple of hours, and he would fix me up.

I went to the bank to cash my check, then picked up a half ounce of pot, and drank three or four beers. (I had stopped in Kansas on the way from Minnesota, and got two 30-packs of six-point beer).

I finally got a call at about 5:00 p.m. on my cell phone. "It's ready, and it's killer".

It was just a couple of miles away. When I got there, he had a couple of lines already laid out for me, so I indulged. He told me that the last batch was in the dehumidifier. He said that

To Hell and Beyond

he had to keep it cool or it would gel up, it was so fresh. It was pink, and it smelled bad, but I took it home; and as soon as I got it home, I went to my room.

It was 6:30 by then, and "Wheel of Fortune" was on. I told my wife to get ready, because we were going to a party.

A single buddy of mine had a big party house just east of Catoosa. We were going out there to play pool with some wannabe pool players. I knew I had the stuff that would let me clean house.

I got out my mirror, my blade, and my straw, and commenced to lay out a couple of lines a half inch wide and two inches long; one for me and one for my wife. This stuff was burning my eyes, and had my whole room smelling.

I leaned over my bed and snorted a line. I slowly sat up on the bed, with my eyes watering and nose burning, like on fire. I stared at the television for about five minutes. I don't even think that I took a breath. As my senses came to me, I mustered up a "Wow".

I thought "If *one* would do that, what would another one do?"

So I leaned over and did the other one too. I sat up on the edge of the bed, and grabbed the bedspread with both hands and held on. I looked at my television. The room got dark, and the T.V. took off.

~ 32 ~

I was left falling weightless, going down. I found that I could stop myself from falling, and did so twice on the way down. This hole seemed to be bottomless. I looked up and saw a small bit of light. It could have been my bedroom light or the television. I continued to descend deeper, and finally reached the bottom.

Because of the low "ceiling", I had to bend down slightly. I looked out at a nasty lake with a shoreline that was oily and dirty. An orange and red fire was burning in the distance across the way. Explosion tracers were coming towards me, and going in all directions. It would die down, then another bunch of gas would come and ignite the flames again and again.

I knew this had to be Hell, and I wondered where the devil was. When I saw him, I thought he must be about seven feet tall. He was in a crouched position. He had long, greasy, jet black hair. He had a real hairy body. He had a ten or twelve foot long tail behind him that would encircle his back side. He was hurt. Torn flesh was hanging from his cheek.

He was making his way toward me, trying to intimidate me. He was going to steal my life, and devour me. He came to kill and destroy me in the lake of fire.

I remember going to the coffee shop with Pastor John after he had prayed for my dad. He told me that the devil wants me, and that the Bible says that he comes to "steal, kill and destroy".

That scripture was now coming to pass.

I remembered what Pastor John said that God could do for me.

I screamed "God help me!"

At that moment, a very huge arm came around me and wrapped around my chest. I looked at it, and it looked like my arm, only larger. All at once, we lifted off at jet speed. The next thing I knew, I was sitting on my bed.

My wife came running into the bedroom. She wanted to know what I was screaming about.

I answered, "We're going to church Sunday".

She asked, "Why?"

I said, "I have been to Hell and back, and I'm not going back again. I want everything out of this house that doesn't pertain to Jesus Christ".

I had never used Christ's name before, unless it was in vain. I had spent 36 years leading myself to Hell, and never saw it coming.

My wife left the room, and told the kids that I was losing it.

I gave her the stuff, and told her to flush it down the toilet, which she did.

Somehow, I had my dad's Bible in my hands, and was clutching it to my body. My sister, Sandy, had given it to me after the funeral. I had it hidden in my room. I didn't want anyone to see it.

I cried out to the Lord, asking Him what was going on. I knew it was Him who had saved me down there.

I said, "Please tell me. Is it you?"

I heard Him say, "Isaiah 41:10".

I looked in the Bible, and really didn't know where Isaiah was, but I found it.

It said, "Fear not, I am with you. Be not dismayed for I am thy God. I will strengthen thee and I will help thee. I will uphold thee with my right hand of righteousness".

It was that right arm that came around me when I was about to get thrown into the lake of fire.

I cried out, "Thank you Lord! But what am I to do? I don't want to go to rehab, or A.A., or N.A.".

He spoke to me and said these words, "You must remove all of the evil things that hinder you. Hence, you will be reckoned. A day of reckoning, and your house will be cleansed, and your shame will be brought forth".

I didn't know what any of that meant, so I wrote it down. I just recently got a computer, and looked up some of the words.

"Removing all evil things", meant all of the paraphernalia that went with the drugs. It meant bongs, papers, glass mirrors, and canisters where we kept our pot. It meant all of our x-rated movies, my pool trophies (approximately fifty), and my NASCARs, because I was high when I won every one of them.

I didn't realize that the Bible say we are not to idolize anything, but to worship God only.

I brought a backhoe home from work, and destroyed everything. I even had some x-rated magazines. If it didn't pertain to Jesus, we didn't need it in our house.

Remove all things that *hinder* you.

*"And he said unto them **hinder** me not, seeing the Lord hath prospered my way. Send me away that I may go to my master."* Genesis 24:56.

*"Ye did run well, who did **hinder** that ye should not obey the truth?"* Galatians 5:7.

*"Don't let your prayers be **hindered**."* I Peter 3:7.

I pulled up 24 scriptures about hindrances, without any problem. Basically, a hindrance is anything that keeps you from God.

The Lord used the word "hence" when He spoke to me, I had no idea what that meant.

*"And the man said they all departed **hence** for I heard them say, 'Let us go to Dothan'."* Genesis 37:17.

In Exodus 11:1, it talks about when Moses was trying to leave Egypt. God told him, *"When I bring the plague upon Pharaoh, he will surely thrust you out **hence**"*.

I didn't realize that "hence" was used in the Bible 63 times. In some verses, He says, *"Hence, get away from your wicked ways"*.

To me it meant to get away from drugs and alcohol.

And then there's "you will be reckoned", and "have a reckoning". It means: ancient of days, chronology, day, hour, seventy weeks, and tabernacle.

It also is the root word for "recognize". People will recognize me by the expression and character of my face.

*"In the sense of Eternal, in contrast with all earthly kings, His days are past **reckoning**."* Daniel 7:9.

*"They were in one **reckoning**, according to their father's house."* I Chronicles 23:11.

The next thing that the Lord had told me, was, my "house must be cleansed". There are a total of 39 scriptures on cleansing.

*"Verily, I have **cleansed** my heart in vain and washed my hands in innocence."* Psalms 73:13.

"Jesus cleansed the leper." Matthew 8:3.

He said that my "shame would be brought forth". There are 111 scriptures dealing with being ashamed. The meaning of 'my shame brought forth' is simple. It's my testimony.

To you, my testimony is a testament of what God can do if you cry out to Him. Even from the pits of Hell, He heard my cry. My wife said it shook the house. I think what shook the house, was that angel of the Lord that entered our house. He brought me home, shoved my dad's Bible into my ribs, and blasted off.

Chapter 6

Guy Gets Saved

The voice of the Lord was very clear to me that day. He said I didn't need rehab. I needed the Word. I know it now, as the 'sword of the Spirit'. I buried it deep into my heart. I was like my father. Every spare minute, I was reading the Bible.

I had been in a bar fight in 1977, over twenty years ago. My left eye was blinded, put out by a glass shoved in my face. I had over eighty stitches in my eyeball. I could only see colors; and letters if they were bigger than two inches. It hurt and watered all of the time, and caused a strain on my other eye.

About 48 hours after I had been to Hell, I woke up and wanted to read. I started at the front of the Bible. I had gotten to late Genesis or early Exodus, when I heard the Lord say, "Matthew".

So I started reading Matthew. For some reason, I skipped over to the ninth chapter, and there it was. Jesus was healing two blind guys. He didn't know them, but they followed Him, and He had compassion on them.

I woke my wife, who understood. I told her that Jesus wanted to heal my eyesight. I prayed that He would heal my sight. My wife stood with me, holding my hand.

He did it! I could now read with both eyes. I read 168 pages before I turned out the light.

You see, He healed me because I was following Him. If you follow Him, He will heal you too!

The next morning was Sunday. I woke up early to read the Bible. I wanted to be ready. Today, I was going to get saved. I thought that I should go to the church where my dad went. It was close, just around the corner, and I was acquainted with Pastor John.

My wife, my daughter, and I walked into the church, and it felt funny, but good. It was almost like my dad was there or something. It was a happy time.

We sat down. People were coming up to us, asking who we were. I told them I was Mac's son, Guy. They thought I had been there before, but I let them know I had not. They told me that I was sitting in my dad's seat.

At that moment, I almost lost it. There was no way I could have known. Some of them said he was probably looking down at me right then. I really don't know how I was guided to that seat. I just knew that was the place where we belonged.

As we waited for Pastor John, this other guy named Joe took the pulpit. He announced that Pastor John was in Kansas, preaching at his son's church; and he had come to teach Ephesians, chapter six.

I didn't know how to find that in the Bible. I had hoped that he would have taught from Matthew or Mark, because what he taught wasn't about getting saved.

My wife, my daughter, and I still said "amen" a bunch of times. The church people thought that we were scholars, like we had been in church all of our lives.

It was, however, a very interesting chapter about putting on the armor of God. He was a real good teacher. As he ended, he simply said, "Well that's it".

At that time, my spirit cried out. I was thinking to myself, "Please Lord, I don't think I can make it another day".

Then Joe shouted, "Wait just a minute! The Lord has told me that someone needs to find Him".

He then leaned over on the pew in front of us. He was gazing over our heads, and out into the crowd. That's when I stood up and almost bumped into him.

He then declared, "You".

We had said "amen" so many times, that he thought we were well on our way to being saints; but all three of us went to the altar. We didn't have far to go since we were sitting in the second row.

Joe led us in the sinner's prayer. He asked if we wanted to get filled with the Holy Spirit.

I said, "What's that?"

To which he replied, "Speaking in tongues".

At that time, my wife said I was already doing that in my sleep. The angel of the Lord must have filled me, so my wife and daughter received the baptism of the Holy Spirit, and the party was on!

Joe informed us that Pastor John would be there that evening and we were excited. I was so glad that we could have church Sunday morning, Sunday night, and Wednesday. I don't feel that I could have gone over three or four days without being in the house of the Lord.

We went home and couldn't wait to get back that night to see Pastor John. As we walked into church that night, he met us with open arms. He was very glad to see us.

Everybody there was glad to see us. The people in that church, were so nice and warmhearted. I talked to several who had been delivered from drugs and alcohol. I wasn't alone. It was such a good feeling.

Now, I was equipped to save the world! We kept going to church, and kept going forward at altar calls. It was a hard struggle, but I didn't want to go back to where I had come from. You see, Hell is no place for anyone.

Chapter 7

My New Life

A couple of weeks later, I was sitting in the break room at work, listening to all of the profanity. These were words that I had frequently used as much or more than any of them, but it was different now. It was piercing my soul.

Fred, the biker dude, was the only one other Christian. He was my go to guy, and he went to Victory Christian Center. Fred said that I would get used to it. He did, and it took him about two years. I was choking, and it had only been two weeks!

I turned my keys in, and quit the job I had worked at for almost twenty years.

That was on a Wednesday, and we had church that night. I needed to talk to Pastor John. I told him I had quit my job, and he said not to worry.

I was strapped for money, but I reached into my pocket and gave $40 of the $60 that I had. Pastor John prayed with me, and I really felt peace about it as I was going home.

When I got home at about 9:30, the phone rang. It was a friend who wanted a pool dug. I told him I didn't even have a backhoe. He said he would rent one, and give me $400 cash for the dig. He knew my job situation. He had spoken to Fred, and got my number from him.

Nobody knew how much I had given, but I remember hearing Pastor John say later that we would receive a ten-fold return on our giving to the Lord.

I got that pool dug in about four and a half hours, and I tried to give half of the money back, but he wouldn't accept it.

He said, "…And lose my blessing? no way!"

I didn't understand that then, like I do now.

The next day I started a new company, G&G Services. My son, son-in-law, and I did real good for about a year.

I was renting the backhoe from a friend. He was such a nice guy, that I went to work for him. I really loved my job. The guys that I worked with were Christians, and always smiling.

Not long after that, I got a call from Fred. He said the preacher at Victory wanted me to come and give my testimony.

He was the preacher that I met while digging a pool at the camp.

I went to Victory that Sunday morning at the Mabee Center. I was walking down the aisle when they called my name, so I came on up to the stage. Pastor Billy Joe introduced me, and I commenced to give my testimony. When I got through, the band started playing and we were ushered out the side door.

They took us across the street to their next service, and I gave my testimony there. When I finished, the band started playing again, and again I was ushered out. They asked me to come back to the Mabee Center for the last service, which I gladly did.

I did not realize that they had given an altar call after I left. They said that they had a terrific response. They wanted me to stay and pray for others.

The pastor invited about twenty of his staff to come forward, and wow, before I knew it, there were between 100 and 200 people that came up. Some were there to receive Jesus and be prayed for. There were some drug abusers and others with marijuana addictions who were delivered that day. Praise Jesus!

Later, Billy Joe, his wife Sharon, and I were talking, and he said that he would like to put my testimony into a sermon.

About six months went by, and I received a phone call. Billy Joe wanted to do a filming with another well known pastor. It would be titled, "From Here to Eternity".

I have always cried when I gave my testimony. I thought I could get through it this time, but even the girl that ran the camera was in tears.

Pastor Billy Joe said the response was huge. A year later, they ran it again. He said it would be seen around the world. Millions of people would see the impact that my experience had on me, as well as many others. It was such an honor.

Chapter 8

Miracles

One day I took my wife to work. It was raining, so I was off that day. I didn't have a lot to do, so I thought I would go to the local bookstore and hang out with some Christians. I was there listening to some CDs and had picked some out to buy, when my cell rang. It was my wife, telling me that her niece had her baby, but there were complications and the baby could die. It was a baby girl named Bailey.

It was important that I start praying right then. The baby was being transported to a nearby hospital. I bought a prayer cloth and a cross pendant for her crib.

I was soon at the hospital, and before I knew it, there was a two ton ambulance backing up to the door. The baby was in a life support capsule. The light was off, and I couldn't even see the baby inside. I laid my hand on the capsule and prayed.

A radiant light shined upon the capsule, and the nurse

who was helping, started to cry. The prayer was simple and the light was God. That's why the nurse was crying. I knew God was there, and that the baby was healed. They had said she was suffering from heart and lung problems. I looked into the capsule and she looked straight at me. Chills went up my spine. Wow, the power of God!

The baby's mom was crying. I handed her the prayer cloth and the cross pendant, and told them I would be back later.

I was touching my Bible and thanking God out loud as I was leaving the hospital.

A nurse yelled across the parking lot, "You are doing a good work young man".

I said, "Thank you Ma'am", and continued to praise the Lord for what He had done.

I picked up my wife and told her what happened. We both went back to the hospital. As we approached the window, I noticed the nurse who had spoken to me. She went to the phone in the nursery and asked me if I was Bailey's uncle.

I told her I was, and she said, "Are you the one that was here praying for her?"

I replied, "Yes".

She said that the doctors have examined her and can find nothing wrong with her. The baby went home three days later. We know that the child was healed by a miracle of God.

The baby's daddy was in prison, so I decided that I would buy her the things she needed. As she was growing up, I would buy her things on her birthdays and such. I didn't see her a lot, but when I did, she would come and stand by my side.

It felt a little strange or maybe, not. It was like somehow she knew that I was there when God breathed that breath of life into her.

The next miracle was during a storm that came through our town of Broken Arrow. I was sitting and reading the Bible, when I looked out and saw a school bus hitting its brakes.

I darted out the door, and there was a funnel touching the ground about 100 feet from me and the bus.

I yelled, "I rebuke you in the name of Jesus!"

The funnel went back into the clouds. The school bus driver stood in amazement. He got in the bus and traveled on his way.

I got in my truck and headed east. The tornado came back down about a mile east of my mobile home, and caused a lot of damage. I praised the Lord for sparing my house and that school bus full of kids. There were no deaths caused by that tornado.

I have seen many more miracles since then. The bottom line is, if you follow Jesus, you will see miracles too.

In the Bible it says that thousands of people followed Jesus, and they were healed.

Chapter 9

Ministry

Jesus has continued to bless me time after time. I can't begin to thank Him enough. I had battled the addiction of marijuana since I was fourteen years old. I had spent thirty-something years, and close to half a million dollars getting high.

Things are so different for us now. I drive a new truck, and my wife drives a nice van. Recently, I bought my daughter a Town and Country van. I paid cash for it, and have money in the bank.

You see, I had done some work for a Christian man in Pryor. He asked me to come and work for him, and I told him that he probably couldn't pay me enough.

He asked me what I was tithing per week.

I told him $100.

He replied, "So I will start you at $1000 a week".

The first year, I made $52,000. The second year, I made $66,000. He started paying me $37.50 an hour for overtime. This year, I made $77,000 gross.

I gave to four different ministries. The more I gave, the more God gave back.

I started giving into a men's ministry with Ed, a friend of mine. There were five other men besides me. Then there were twelve. I started giving them $100 a month for a breakfast we would have once a month.

Things just started to snowball, and we began getting more and more work for my boss. We kept having our monthly breakfast for the men, and soon we had 25 men showing up in this small church in Catoosa.

We prayed for fifty, and soon we had 54 at our breakfast. We would always have a good time and a small service after our meal.

Last month, we had 84 men. We had rib-eye steaks, and pork chops, and chicken, all grilled. We also had sausage, bacon, scrambled eggs, potatoes, and biscuits and gravy.

We eat at 8:00 a.m., and preach at 8:30 a.m., and are out by 9:15 a.m. We meet on the second Saturday of every month.

We have already started another one at another church. Two more, and we will have one every week of the month.

In two short years, the Lord has shown us that if you feed them, they will come. We are expecting 100 this coming Saturday. I get so blessed seeing hands go up for salvation. A lot of these guys are bikers, and have their own ministry too. We love them. We feed them. We plant the seeds, and they grow.

I have been told that there are men's ministries sprouting up all over.

Now I know what the Lord meant when He said that as long as the earth remains, there will be seedtime and harvest. The fields are wide, and the harvest is plenty.

I don't know where I would have been right now if it weren't for the Lord. I do know that I died that night. My body was shut down, and I was down for the count. Why I was chosen, why I was given this one more chance, I'll never know. I do know that it's not the Lord's will for anyone to perish.

I give the Lord total credit for what has happened to me. I don't know if He goes into Hell and looks for us. I do know that on March 17, 2000 I was saved from a terrible fate.

I know that my dad had asked people at church to pray for me, and I know he is smiling down at me. He read the Bible daily, and now I am following in his footsteps.

Make sure that when you pick a church, it has a backbone. Make sure they teach and preach the whole Bible.

Acts, chapter two comes to mind. Without the Holy Spirit I would just be another person sitting there, going through the motions. God wants us to get excited about the Holy Spirit, to sing loud, and to praise and worship the Lord.

The Bible says that the Word is like a two-edged sword. One edge is reading the Word. The other edge is speaking the Word.

Our Lord likes for us to witness and testify. It helps others to see the error of their ways.

I began asking the Lord to save 100 souls. Then I asked the Lord to save thousands, and now I am asking for millions to be saved across the globe.

My prayer for you is that you would be saved, get into a good Bible-based church, and be filled with the Holy Spirit!

God will bless you, like He has me. I was a real heathen. I didn't just start fights. I ended them. Now I am fighting for you and yours and millions of others.

I can't testify to what Heaven is like, but I know that Hell is no place I want to spend eternity.

Praise the Lord for all of His goodness. Let everything that has breath, praise the Lord.

Get saved.

Love ya always,
Guy McAnally

Chapter 10

A Final Word

I would like to take this time to bring you up to date. As I gaze across the land, I find that there are still a lot of hurting people. As I speak and share the Word, I sense a cry, if you will. People without Jesus are in a constant battle with none other than Satan himself.

Saints, we have got to stand our ground. We have to start our day by reading the Word of God. Ephesians 6:13 says that we must put on the whole armor of God, because it's the only way to quench the fiery darts of the wicked one.

I hate to tell you, but the devil is still around, and he's still stealing, killing, and destroying all he touches. If you are having trouble with him, try this: Read Ephesians 6:11 through verse 24. It will take you less than two minutes. It's all about warfare. Put on the armor of God. Gird your loins with truth. Put on the breast plate of righteousness, with your feet shod with the preparation of peace. Above all, take the shield of faith. Then you shall be able to quench the firey darts of the wicked. Take the helmet of salvation and the sword of the Spirit, which is the Word of God, the Bible.

Just as I was writing this, my wife Barbara fell and did a flip off of our front porch. What did I do? I got up, rebuked the devourer, Satan, and I prayed. She was crying. She thought her arm was broken.

I yelled, "No! In the name of Jesus, no bones will be broken".

I broke out the ice pack. She had skinned her arm from top to bottom. I said, "No blood will be shed, just the blood that Jesus already shed at Calvary".

Now you can believe me or not. Did my wife go to the doctor? No. She believed God, and was healed. Thank you, Jesus.

I told this because it really happened, and it just goes to show you that disaster can strike at any time. It's how you battle it that determines the outcome. Oh by the way, my wife just went out, got in her van and went to my daughter's house to pick up her kids; two boys and a precious, sweet little girl, Lexiona.

I'm not partial, but we just don't have many girls. They are all cute. We have thirteen grandkids and eight of them are boys.

You folks, God loves you so much. He gave His only Son. In Isaiah 54 and 55, he foretold the birth, death, and resurrection, 600 years before it happened. I said that to say this: Jesus knew why He came, to go to the cross. Did he run from His problem? No. He ran to the solution, the cross. Isaiah says the He was bruised for our iniquity. That's putting it lightly. He was slaughtered. But the stone of His tomb was rolled away, and I came to say that He lives!

He lives. He's omnipresent, omnipotent (just like that sweet perfume that you ladies wear). He is right where you are. All you have to do is reach out and touch the hem of His garment. Sometimes we have to turn a little. We may have to get up, or maybe down, prostrate on the floor. Get out of your comfort zone.

The Bible says that if we confess our sins, that Jesus is a just God, and He will forgive us of our sins. John the Baptist called Him the Lamb of God, the One that came to take away the sins of the world.

Look at me. I'm nobody special. I just recognize the hand of God when I see it, and I welcome Him to come and dwell with me. I can feel His presence right now, and so can you.

Don't worry about the tears if you cry. Don't be embarrassed. This is God that we're talking about. The Bible says that He takes our tears and keeps them in a bottle. I never used to cry about anything, but now that I have returned from Hell, I cry every time I turn around. I cry every time I see someone get saved, even if I don't know them.

If you would have known me before, you would know that I was bad. I was in jail once for nearly killing a guy. I'm here to tell you that when you get saved, you change from the inside out. I used to fly off the handle at the drop of a hat. I'm speaking to you, reader. With God's help, you can beat this thing, or whatever your problem is.

I'm inspired to write this book for one reason and one reason alone. It's you, the reader.

God speaks and I write. I've had nine years to do this book. Three years ago I was given a prophecy. A year ago, it was prophesied that I should about my life changing experience. I did nothing. Two weeks ago, I ran into the guy that spoke those words to me. He was excited to ask me if I had written my book yet. I had to tell him no. He told me that I didn't get it, and he was ticked off that I hadn't done anything.

He then looked me in the eyes and said to write the book. So here it is.

You see, God sent His prophets to me for a reason. The reason is you!

I was too busy. Well, it's been raining for three weeks, and I work outside. I finally got the hint. OK Lord Jesus.

For all of the blessings He has given me, I'm forever grateful. I hate to say it, but sometimes we forget where we came from.

Lord, I confess that I've been guilty of that, and I'm sorry, but I'm on fire once again. Thank you for encouraging me, Jesus.

Thank you, reader. I pray that you will be inspired to walk with the Lord as I have. The keys are simple. Read the Word daily. Get in a Bible-based church. If you read the prayer in Ephesians 6:11 through verse 24 every day and get it down in your spirit, you can take authority over the devil. You can actually start to get some of your stuff back that the snake stole from you. Job got ten times what the devil stole from him, and that's my prayer for you.

The Bible says that if you will hunger and thirst for righteousness, He will call you blessed. I don't know about you, but I'll take that. All you have to do is to claim it right now in the name of Jesus. I think you're about to get a hold of this thing.

If my dad, my mom, my grandma, and my dad's little Victory Church hadn't prayed; the devil would have devoured me, but God had another plan.

God wants you to be humble. The Bible says that if we humble ourselves and pray, then He will heal our land. I'm just one man, but so was Jesus. He keeps reminding me of how populated the world is. That's why we have books like this to read, and things like Bible Gateway on the internet.

There is no reason for a man or woman to be unhappy. Find Jesus, then all of these things that you need will be added to you.

If you have a television and satellite service, you will find that there are about twelve Christian channels, with good preaching and good gospel music. What more could you possibly need?

Do you want a Christian mate? Try church. Pray that the Lord will send you one, and He will. All you have to do is ask.

In Mark 11:23 it says that our words can move mountains. In verse 24, he says that whatever we ask when we pray, to believe that we shall have it. Now, I don't know of too many Corvettes that God has handed out, but I do know of one, and a whole bunch of Harley Davidson motorcycles; as well as cars, houses, land, food, and lots of favor.

If you are a child of the King, you can have what you desire, just like the scripture says. Just remember to thank the Lord every time. The more you thank Him, the more you will have.

You know, the way I got my job was by tithing and giving. Hey wait a minute! Don't hang up. I'm trying to tell you how to get blessed.

Anyway, I had seen a man named Leroy. He's a black guy with a real anointing. I was in the audience, and he looked at me.

He said, "Hey you, construction worker, you fifty dollar a week tither. I'm going to tell you how to increase your $400 or $500 dollar pay".

He was preaching right to me. Don't get me wrong. I had been giving and was getting blessed, but I felt I was getting anywhere, so when they passed the plate I stepped up and gave my first $100 offering. A year later, I was making about $900 a week.

Still, I wasn't quite there. I had done some work for a guy named Alvin from Pryor, Oklahoma. He's a solid Christian. When he asked me what I was tithing each week, I told him $100. He actually paid me $1000 a week, based on what I was tithing, thanks to Jesus and Leroy, a black man on fire for God, prophesying to a white man. Isn't God good?

I said that to say this: If you have trouble with any race issues, you are in a world of hurt. You need prayer. Heaven will be filled with all races.

I have friends of every race, even Muslim friends at the corner store. I preach to them about the love of God all the time. I try to show them the way. They know I am blessed by what I drive. A couple of times, I have made up what people were short paying for groceries, nothing big, just out of the ordinary. Now I see them doing it every time. I thank the Lord for them.

The nice things that you do will stand in God's kingdom, and it catches on. Amen! Wow. I'm about to preach myself happy here. You're light doesn't have to be bright to make a difference in a dark room. Just a little kindness is better than none at all.

I wouldn't want you to get excited or anything, but come on, try the waters. You can wade in as deep as you want. Let's face it. All I'm selling here is eternal life. The Lord has sustained me, and I'm trying to get you in on the ground floor. It's a front row seat to worship the King of kings and Lord of lords.

If you get to church early, there's nobody on the front row. The music is loud. Raise your hands with the anointing flowing from the presence of the Lord. If there's anything you need, just praise Him and it's yours.

This is a sermon that I wrote to you, just for purchasing my book. I do hope you were blessed by it.

Oh, my wife still has no pain. Praise God. He's so good.

Bye for now. I hope you are blessed. I send my love to all of you saints and sinners, because God raised me from my SIN for such a time as this. Praise God!

Love always,

Guy McAnally

To contact Guy McAnally:

E-mail: gbmac2009@gmail.com

Made in the USA
Monee, IL
06 July 2020